2017 PROPHETIC FORECAST

DOUG ADDISON

2017 Prophetic Forecast
By Doug Addison

Printed in USA by InLight Connection
PO Box 7049, Santa Maria, CA 93456

For ordering information contact: InLight Connection (800) 507-7853
To order: DougAddison.com

Cover Design by Christian Wetzel

Book design by Treasure Image & Publishing
TreasureImagePublishing.com (248) 403-8046

ENDORSEMENTS

2017 will undoubtedly be an unprecedented year! Doug Addison's *2017 Prophetic Forecast* beautifully highlights prophetic insights and the milestones that we hope to reach in the upcoming year.

This encouraging book is both practical and inspiring, as Doug gives you prayer strategies while awakening hope for a victorious year. It truly is an impartation of vision and you won't want to miss it!

Kris Vallotton
Leader, Bethel Church, Redding, CA
Co-Founder of Bethel School of Supernatural Ministry
Author of eleven books, including
The Supernatural Ways of Royalty and *Spirit War*
KrisVallotton.com

I was already excited about the year 2017 as God has been speaking many positive things to me about this year we are entering into. But now, having just finished reading Doug Addison's *2017 Prophetic Forecast*, I guess I would now have to tell you that I'm "SUPER EXCITED!" about 2017!

This is going to be great ... partnering with Heaven in these months we are now entering. God is about to blow the doors off of our current mindsets in how we reach the lost, participate in revival, and in fact in how we do life itself.

Steve Shultz
Founder of The Elijah List
ElijahList.com

I read Doug's *Daily Prophetic Words* every day and I am really excited to have the prophetic word for this year in one book! It is a confirmation of what God is showing me for this new year. This is a year of going out with the old and in with the new. I am excited about what lies ahead for the Church in 2017 and beyond.

Joan Hunter
Author and President of Joan Hunter Ministries
JoanHunter.org

Doug Addison has done it again! He has compiled this *2017 Prophetic Forecast* that gives believers a bright hope and plan for a successful future. We can expect great and glorious things to happen in 2017.

This anointed manuscript is full of faith, prophetic wisdom and timing that will empower you to embrace the changes that are necessary to be part of revival.

Dr. Barbie L. Breathitt
Founder of Breath of the Spirit Ministries, Inc.
BarbieBreathitt.com

I want to recommend my friend Doug Addison's latest book, *2017 Prophetic Forecast.*

Doug does a great job of going into visions and revelation from past seasons and years and bringing them forward into 2017.

As I read through the book I received wave after wave after wave of hope and encouragement with every new scope of revelation that was brought.

Johnny Enlow
Author of *Seven Mountain Prophecy*
and *Seven Mountain Renaissance*
JohnnyAndElizabeth.com

When the church needs to hear the word of the Lord, God always sends Doug Addison to let us know what He is saying for that season.

In *2017 Prophetic Forecast,* Doug brings forth the timing of the Lord when God will initiate 'open windows and doors' for the greater portion of His glory in the earth!

Doug is a prophet who is compassionate, loving and anointed in this hour to bring forth the ministry of reconciliation and restoration. This book is a must for those who have an ear to hear and an eye to see!

Dr. Jeremy Lopez
Founder and President of Identity Network International
IdentityNetwork.net

God does nothing without first revealing it to his prophetic people. God has released to Doug some of His secrets about amazing events that are about to occur. *2017 Prophetic Forecast* is the real deal and a must-read to be ready for what is coming!

Dr. David Herzog
Founder, David Herzog Ministries
Author of *Glory Invasion*, *Mysteries of the Glory*, and *Aligning with Heaven*
TheGloryZone.org

A fire will burn within you as you absorb Doug Addison's captivating new book: *2017 Prophetic Forecast*. For those who are seeing the glass half empty, get ready to see the glass overflow with new hope for the New Year. Doug's prophetic forecast includes both physical and spiritual weather patterns, with the certain possibility of sunshine piercing through dark clouds.

Bill Yount
Blowing The Shofar Ministry
Author of *Some Hear Thunder ... I Hear A Roar!: Supernatural Encounters & Stories to Encourage Your Heart*
BillYount.com

Doug Addison has done it again. His prophecies ring true. His new book, *2017 Prophetic Forecast*, is a great encouragement and blueprint for what God is about to do in your life and mine in 2017. Read it and be encouraged!

Wendy Griffith
700 Club Co-host & CBN News Anchor

CONTENTS

INTRODUCTION

There is a time each year that is important for your life because it prophetically sets the course for the upcoming year. It is the time between the Jewish New Year, called *Rosh Hashanah* (October 2–4, 2016) and *Yom Kippur*, or Day of Atonement (October 11–12, 2016). Even though we are no longer under the Law of Moses, God still operates on the Jewish calendar.

Historically, Jewish people believe that God examines our lives during the time between Rosh Hashanah and Yom Kippur to see if we are ready for spiritual advancement or promotion to a new level of maturity. Whether you are aware of it or not, this is a time when you are able to hear God more clearly and gain direction. The ten days between Rosh Hashanah and Yom Kippur are called the *Days of Awe*.

Our Lives Are Examined Each Year

Here is what is written about this time in Wikipedia.com:

"According to Jewish tradition, God inscribes each person's fate for the coming year into a book, the Book of Life, on Rosh Hashanah, and waits until Yom

Kippur to 'seal' the verdict. During the Days of Awe, a Jew tries to amend his or her behavior and seek forgiveness for wrongs done against God ... and against other human beings....[i]

The evening before and the day of Yom Kippur are set aside for public and private petitions and confessions of guilt. At the end of Yom Kippur, one hopes that they have been forgiven by God."

We no longer have to atone for our own sins because that was done for us through Jesus on the Cross. But God opens the Book of Life over us all each year during the time of Rosh Hashanah, Yom Kippur and the Feast of Tabernacles.

Here is a recap of the process that happens each year. God examines our lives during the Jewish New Year (Rosh Hashanah). Ten days later, He seals our verdict on the Day of Atonement (Yom Kippur). Then God reveals the results 11 days later, on the last day of the Feast of Tabernacles, also called *Hoshanah Rabbah*.

This is a total of 22 days. You can read more about these Jewish holidays in Leviticus 16, Leviticus 23:23–44, Numbers 29:1–6 and Deuteronomy 16:13–16.

Heavenly Books Opened

Further study shows us in Daniel 7:10b that there are books or scrolls in Heaven that are opened, and the Courts of Heaven review them. These books can be about us personally, as in Psalm 139:16, or about greater global issues. They contain blueprints and strategies needed to advance the Kingdom of God in our lives and on Earth.

From a prophetic standpoint, the New Year begins on the last day of Rosh Hashanah, which for 2016 was on October 4th. Most people, however, operate based on the Gregorian calendar, in which the New Year begins on January 1st of each year.

I am writing this book from the standpoint of both. Since most people are used to the Gregorian calendar, I release prophetic words on my blog for the year starting in January. However, I am writing this *2017 Prophetic Forecast* based on what I am hearing God say starting after Rosh Hashanah, October 2016, through the next Jewish New Year which will be September 20–22, 2017.

Why I Am Writing This Book

My calling from God is to help people understand how God is speaking through a *now-prophetic word.* A now-prophetic word is something that can be applied to your life right now to encourage you and give you guidance. It is not usually intended for a time in the future but, as it says—it is for *now*.

These are prophetic words that talk about the timing of God. For a number of years, I have released daily, weekly and monthly prophetic words of direction. I have found that timing and now-prophetic words are sometimes hard to put in a book. They are often like *manna*, which was food from Heaven given to the Israelites. It was good for one day and went away after that.

This all changed for me after I had a spiritual experience on April 25, 2015. I was awakened early in the morning to a vision of an angel handing me a shepherd's staff. I knew it was a gift coming to me that would allow me to *shepherd* the prophetic words I was getting.

I knew that what I was receiving was similar to what the late Seer-Prophet Bob Jones used to call his *Shepherd's Rod*. Bob's *Shepherd's Rod* was an annual book that he would publish containing prophetic insights for the coming year. I was friends with and mentored by Bob Jones, so I was at his house and heard some of the stories firsthand of how God spoke to him.

Prophet Bobby Connor also releases a *Shepherd's Rod* each year describing prophetic words that God speaks to him on Yom Kippur.

Over the last few years, I have had some encounters and God has given me specific prophetic words for the upcoming year. Last year was the first time I released prophetic words for the year. I shared these in the *2016 Prophetic Forecast* book. I got a lot of positive feedback about the accuracy of the revelation in that book. This book, *2017 Prophetic Forecast,* is my second annual prophetic forecast.

I have been releasing prophetic words on my blog for over a decade. Because I release so many prophetic words, they can often be forgotten. Putting them together in book form allows people to remember and pray about them. It also helps bring the pieces together and paints a fuller picture of what God is saying.

"Then the Lord replied: 'Write down the revelation and make it plain on tablets so that a herald may run with it.'" Habakkuk 2:2

God speaks in so many ways, yet many people can easily miss it. One thing that Jesus often taught through the parables is that in the Kingdom of God we must have *"eyes that see and ears that hear"* (Matthew 13:16).

He was talking about seeing and hearing spiritual things so that we may come to know His voice in deeper ways. God truly is speaking all the time, but most people are either missing or not understanding what is being said to them. I base the prophetic words and writing I do on Ephesians 1:17–19a:

"I keep asking that the God of our Lord Jesus Christ, the glorious Father, may give you the Spirit of wisdom and revelation, so that you may know him better. I pray that the eyes of your heart may be enlightened in order that you may know the hope to which he has called you, the riches of his glorious inheritance in his holy people and his incomparably great power for us who believe ..."

The sole purpose of hearing God and the reason I release prophetic words, is so that you may know God better! The closer we get to God, the clearer His voice becomes. The apostle Paul compares God's wisdom and revelation to riches. These are the true riches that God wants to open up to you; namely, the ability to hear His voice and respond.

I also base hearing God and the gift of prophecy on the key principle of encouragement.

"But the one who prophesies speaks to people for their strengthening, encouraging and comfort." 1 Corinthians 14:3

When we hear the Father's voice and begin to offer words to others, the goal is that they would be strengthened, encouraged and comforted. We have been living in a time when there has been an abundance of prophetic words and revelation, but not enough wisdom and understanding about the timing of them. The result of not seeing prophecy fulfilled has brought prophetic disappointments.

"Hope deferred makes the heart sick, but a longing fulfilled is a tree of life." Proverbs 13:12

For a number of years, I have been releasing the *Daily Prophetic Word* as well as weekly and monthly prophetic articles and blogs. My specialty is to understand the times and seasons when it comes to hearing God. Not all the prophetic words I release will apply to everyone. But I am getting feedback from thousands of people about how these words bring confirmation or encouragement to keep going during trying or difficult times.

Some of the prophetic words are based on new things God is speaking to me for 2017. I am also including some prophetic words that were already released on my *Spirit Connection* webcast and blog that are important for this year and I have updated them for 2017. Even though there is a date on this, it does not mean that it is limited to this year.

God operates outside of time, so you can grab hold of any of the prophetic words in this book. Respond by praying and agreeing with God for it in your own life. Please share these words with others because they will help people gain greater insight into what is happening in the world and in our lives.

My hope and prayer is that you will rise above the negative clamor out there about God judging us and that this is the end of the world. Also, I hope that you will come to know God better through the prophetic words, dreams and experiences I am sharing, as well as through your own.

CHAPTER 1

CHANGE IN POLITICAL ATMOSPHERE

"Forget the former things; do not dwell on the past. See, I am doing a new thing! Now it springs up; do you not perceive it? I am making a way in the wilderness and streams in the wasteland." Isaiah 43:18–19

As you read this book, I want to encourage you to try not to view these prophecies through the lens of what it means politically to the United States or to your country. This is important because what God is about to do is outside of our current understanding and paradigm.

God is going to bring about a movement that is no longer limited to the four walls of a church or to a particular political party. He is going to do something so radical that you will be stretched in your understanding of it.

God is building His Kingdom on Earth and what is coming will not fit into our current structure or wineskin.

Prophetic Word for the United States

On November 8, 2016, the morning of the Presidential elections, I got the following prophetic word for the United States.

"O America, I still love you and see your zeal for Me. Satan has asked to sift you like wheat and the enemy has been waging war against you. But a remnant is going to arise to possess the land. Your sons and daughters are going to awaken from a sleep and rise up like a mighty army. They will be like David's mighty men (and women). Yes, women! I am moving on women in this hour. I Am going to do this and it will bring about great changes that are needed for this time. There is a shifting of power and the worldly political religious spirit is falling. From this will rise a fresh new move of My Holy Spirit that cannot be contained. What I am going to do will confound the wise and not be understood through the current beliefs and thinking that many of My people have been holding to. I am going to bring new wine of My power and presence and a new wineskin that will not look like or fit into the old."

Also, the Bible says:

"However, as it is written: 'What no eye has seen, what no ear has heard, and what no human mind has conceived'—

the things God has prepared for those who love him—these are the things God has revealed to us by his Spirit. The Spirit searches all things, even the deep things of God.

For who knows a person's thoughts except their own spirit within them? In the same way no one knows the thoughts of God except the Spirit of God. What we have received is not the spirit of the world, but the Spirit who is from God, so that we may understand what God has freely given us." 1 Corinthians 2:9–12

How to Respond

No matter our religious beliefs, political party affiliations or who we voted for, it is important that those of us in the United States respond biblically to Donald Trump being our new President. Remember that God is still in charge of the world and it is His Kingdom and rule we are under and not man's rule.

The apostle Paul urged us to pray for leaders during a time when the world leaders were not godly. God wants us to pray for leaders no matter their political party or beliefs. We need to pray that God's will is done and not our own desires.

"I urge, then, first of all, that petitions, prayers, intercession and thanksgiving be made for all people—for

kings and all those in authority, that we may live peaceful and quiet lives in all godliness and holiness. This is good, and pleases God our Savior, who wants all people to be saved and to come to a knowledge of the truth." 1 Timothy 2:1–4

God wants all people to be saved. This includes those who have different beliefs and political views. Be at peace and expect God our Father to bring about good things for us. This is part of getting us ready for a new worldwide revival. My desire is to bring peace to you during a time of turmoil and uncertainty. It is important for us to respond with maturity and trust the Lord in the midst of these trying times.

CHAPTER 2

2017 PROPHETIC WORDS

"Praise the Lord, all you nations; extol him, all you peoples. For great is his love toward us, and the faithfulness of the Lord endures forever. Praise the Lord." Psalm 117:1–2

2017 is going to be a time when many nations and people groups begin to awaken to God's love. A long-awaited global awakening, revival and harvest will begin. This is both for the nations of the world and unique people groups from the nations who have been scattered around the world.

The world is going to awaken to the awesome power of the Lord. There is a reason for all the turmoil and attacks. It is the enemy trying to blind us from seeing what God is doing. God is more powerful than Satan, but some people have fallen into the trap of looking at the storms and not to the Lord's solution. As darkness seems to increase around us, God uses these events and circumstances to draw people to Himself.

We are about to see various movements of God that will result in global harvest and revival. Do not be discouraged by how things look in the natural realm. God is moving in our lives right now to align and position us for some amazing things.

Days of Awe 2016

As I mentioned previously in this book, the Jewish New Year, called Rosh Hashanah, was on October 2–4, 2016, and the Day of Atonement, called Yom Kippur, was on October 11–12, 2016. Even though we are no longer under the Law of Moses, God still operates on the Jewish calendar. This is the time each year that is important for your life, because it sets the course for you prophetically for the upcoming year.

This past year, October 2–12, 2016, was the most spiritually active time in Heaven I have ever seen. It extended through October 23, the last day of the Feast of Tabernacles, also known as Hoshanah Rabbah, and it was 22 days of the most powerful encounters in Heaven I have had in my life. At the same time, it was the highest warfare I have ever had in my life!

The Books of Heaven were opened over all of us. But this year, it was a rare occurrence for this to be done by the highest level court in Heaven. I had several experiences in which I saw and heard what I believe was the Daniel 7 Ancient of Days court sessions taking place.

Books of Heaven Being Opened

During the Days of Awe, the Books of Heaven are opened over us. Daniel 7:10 shows us that there are books (or scrolls) in Heaven that are opened and the Courts of Heaven review them. These books can be about us personally, as in Psalm 139:16, or about greater global issues. They contain blueprints and strategies needed to advance the Kingdom of God in our lives and on Earth.

I have had several encounters in the Courts of Heaven over the past year; something special is happening this year. There is a higher-level examination of our lives that is going to bring about new promotions and assignments that will affect the next seven years of our lives. I saw what reminded me of the Daniel 7 Court of Heaven taking place over people.

"As I looked, 'thrones were set in place, and the Ancient of Days took his seat. His clothing was as white as snow; the hair of his head was white like wool. His throne was flaming with fire, and its wheels were all ablaze. A river of fire was flowing, coming out from before him. Thousands upon thousands attended him; ten thousand times ten

thousand stood before him. The court was seated, and the books were opened.'" Daniel 7:9–10

The Lord told me that this is a very rare time, and it is a rare event to have the Ancient of Days court session. It is the highest court and level of authority in Heaven. The Father (Ancient of Days) is rendering decisions and judgments for those who have been called to be part of this next move of God. Many have been over-attacked by the enemy, and have felt they failed or have been forgotten.

The Father in Heaven has been rendering decisions and judgments for those who have been called to be a part of this next move of God and revival. The enemy has retaliated against what God is releasing from Heaven.

This is why we have seen strange weather patterns, storms, fires, floods and earthquakes. There have been high levels of unrest on the Earth because of the battle happening in the heavenly realm right now.

"As I watched, this horn was waging war against the holy people and defeating them, until the Ancient of Days came and pronounced judgment in favor of the holy people of the Most High, and the time came when they possessed the kingdom." Daniel 7:21–22

Get Ready to Possess the Kingdom

God has pronounced judgments and decrees in our favor. He is releasing plans and strategies for us to take hold of the new season and possess the Kingdom on Earth as it is in Heaven. New forerunners are being commissioned and will start coming on the scene soon to prepare us for the next amazing move of God.

God is getting things ready for a new revival geared towards those who have been rejected or wounded by Christians or Christianity in general. Things are beginning now and are lining up for two moves of God. The first will be to refresh and awaken the Church. Many will judge this new move as not being from God.

The second move of God is coming later in 2017, and will be a true revival for the people who are way outside of the Church. These are the Ezekiel 34 *weak sheep* who have been pushed away, forgotten and rejected.

A New Gate in Heaven Opened

Many people have been going through difficult times and we are seeing and feeling a sense of unrest. There has been heavy spiritual warfare, bad weather patterns and attacks of the enemy. In the midst of these difficulties, I want to encourage you to hang on, because something new is coming.

The enemy does not want you to see what it is. He is throwing everything he has to distract you by getting you to look at the storm rather than the solution God is bringing.

"Lift up your heads, O ye gates; and be ye lift up, ye everlasting doors; and the King of glory shall come in." Psalm 24:7 KJV

Something major shifted into place starting in October 2016, as God began releasing new strategies and assistance from Heaven. In the midst of unrest, God opened a new *Gate of Rest* for us to enter into.

To survive and thrive during this time of transition, it is important to get God's perspective and trust that He is still in charge and has not forgotten you. God is inviting you to enter into His rest, where you can find peace during this time of transition.

The Power in Unity

There has been a spirit of disunity and disagreement dominating the world. Disunity has caused us to become ineffective at reaching the world.

When we can agree together, we will touch the heart of God and ultimately come into agreement with God's heart (loving plan) for the Earth. This is going to release blueprints and strategies from Heaven.

"Again, truly I tell you that if two of you on earth agree about anything they ask for, it will be done for them by my Father in heaven." Matthew 18:19

This will bring a much-needed shift in the spiritual atmosphere. Watch for God to reveal things to you that had previously been sealed away. This could be things that He had spoken to you, but you did not understand or you had forgotten. Also, dreams that were hidden away are now coming to the surface.

God is releasing greater understanding, wisdom and deeper knowledge about situations in your life. Pay close attention to this so you do not miss them.

Ask God for Revelation

This is a time of restoration and revelation. The shaking many people are experiencing is designed by God to shake open things that have been previously sealed. Now is the time for the sealed to be revealed.

"Call to me and I will answer you and tell you great and unsearchable things you do not know." Jeremiah 33:3

Know that God is establishing you right now, and you will indeed make it through this time. Many are going to come out of this time in an entirely new place, new level, new authority, anointing and fire! Even though things are shaking, remember that God's Kingdom cannot be shaken!

"Therefore, since we are receiving a kingdom that cannot be shaken, let us be thankful, and so worship God acceptably with reverence and awe, for our 'God is a consuming fire.'" Hebrews 12:28–29

Position Yourself for Something New

It is important to stay in step with God, even if you are not sure what God is calling you to do. What does that look like? Do what you need to do to not give up in tough times. Pray and remind God of the promises you have over your life. Do the practical things that bring you close to God: prayer, worship, communion, reading the Bible, taking walks and connecting with God.

Positioning yourself involves getting deeper healing, growing in intimacy, learning to love and coming into agreement with God's will and ways for your life.

It may also mean changing the people you are hanging around. It is time to move upward so ask God to help you find people who are on the same path.

Get ready to do what it takes to align yourself to receive in this new season. If necessary and God confirms these things, then you can expect to see changes in your living situation, changes in location and jobs, church affiliations, business partners or whatever God shows you. Get ready for change this year!

CHAPTER 3

THE GLORY TRAIN RETURNING IN 2017

In order to understand many of the prophecies in this book and what God is doing this year, it helps to be familiar with two prophecies from the late Seer-Prophet Bob Jones. The first is about the *Billion Soul Revival* and the second is the *Return of the Greater Glory of God* that departed shortly after the Jesus People Movement ended in the 1970s. The return of the greater glory is needed to fulfill Bob's first prophecy about the harvest (revival).

Let me give you a recap of what God is speaking so it does not get lost, because I will be unpacking a lot of details. There is a major revival coming that has been delayed for a number of years. Before this new global-level revival and harvest of souls can happen, we need the glory of God back in the Church at large, not just on some anointed individuals as it is now.

God spoke to me and to Bob Jones' wife, Bonnie, that the glory of God is coming back on the 40th anniversary of when Bob saw it leave in 1977. That will be in March, 2017. Something big is going to start after that time, and it will unfold more and more over the next few years.

Prophet Bob Jones

Bob Jones was one of the most humble and amazingly accurate Seer-Prophets that I have ever met. Bob was one of the Kansas City Prophets in the 1980s, and was instrumental in restoring the prophetic gifts to the Church. I wish I had time in this book to tell you about all the accurate prophecies that Bob released.

For example, in the 1980s he saw Chinese people worshiping the Lord with handheld TV sets (before the invention of the smartphone), which is happening right now. He also predicted a comet, ten years prior to the date, which would come as a confirmation of what God was doing. Most of all, Bob had an incredible love for the Lord and people.

Billion Soul Revival

On August 8, 1975, Bob Jones died and was taken into Heaven to meet Jesus. Instead of being invited in like others in line with him, Jesus sent Bob back to Earth with a mandate to prepare the Church for a major revival of all revivals. The Lord told Bob that there would be a movement on the Earth that will bring in one billion people, and that the majority will be young people who are considered outcasts and offensive to the current Church.

Bob's entire life and ministry was centered around this prophecy. He was known as the prophet of love, and he went back to Heaven on Valentine's Day, February 14, 2014. His passing occurred before he was able to see the start of the revival. But God has never forgotten this prophetic promise and things are now lining up for it to come about.

My Connection to This

As I share this, I want to be clear that what is coming is bigger than one man, woman or ministry can fulfill. I am not saying that I have the mantle of Bob Jones, but we all have a part in it.

I have been around the prophetic movement for many years. I spent the entire decade of the 1990s as a business owner, an undercover prophetic evangelist in San Francisco and a church planter.

In 2001, God captured me with a powerful encounter and mandate. I had just gotten healed of Huntington's Disease, and I left pastoring to pursue a greater call on my life, though I was not yet sure what it was.

I got hold of a videotape of Bob Jones being interviewed by Wesley Campbell at a conference in Kelowna, British Columbia, Canada. The Holy Spirit hit my wife and me with power. God spoke to me that I was being given an assignment to help Bob Jones fulfill his life calling of the Billion Soul Revival that was coming. It seemed farfetched and impossible, but it was the Lord who spoke it!

I was literally out of ministry at the time, an unknown former pastor and struggling business owner. The Lord spoke to me to get ready and sell it all because He was about to move us into our destiny. At age 42, my wife and I had a huge yard sale. We sold everything except our personal belongings and moved to a tiny apartment in Burlingame, California, and waited on the Lord's instructions. Within three months, God gave us a plan.

We moved to New Hampshire and Linda and I joined the staff of John Paul Jackson's Streams Ministries. It was a humbling season and we worked very hard.

A few months later we met Bob Jones and I got to share what God had spoken to me. We started our ministry, InLight Connection, in 2001 with the sole purpose of training people in the prophetic and doing prophetic outreaches. I knew a day would come when we would be part of helping to fulfill Bob's mandate of the Billion Soul Revival.

We moved back to California to pursue this vision. A few years later we bought a prayer cabin and moved to Moravian Falls, North Carolina. During that time, I had the opportunity to mentor with Bob at his house and I traveled to conferences with him and his wife, Bonnie.

As I look back I have to pinch myself to say, "Is this a dream?" How amazing and faithful our God is!

The Glory Needs to Return

The timing of this revival has not been in line with what Bob had originally thought, but that does not make this a false prophecy. Bob knew that the glory power of God had to return to the Church before we could have a revival of this magnitude.

Many things would need to line up. Even if it is God's desire for it to happen, it can be delayed based on how people respond. God will not do anything that we are not ready for.

One thing Bob saw was that without God's greater glory and power, we would not be able to be part of a revival and movement this big. God's glory is a manifest presence of the Holy Spirit that comes upon us. It is greater than the gifts and anointing to do God's work. The glory of God comes like a thick, liquid love and electricity mixed together.

In 1975, the Lord spoke to Bob that the Greater Glory of God was going to leave the Church because it was used for man's gain instead of for revival and the Lord's work. On March 17, 1977, Bob saw this Glory lift from the Church and it has not returned since. Yes, there are people who still carry portions of it, but overall the Glory of God has not been on the Church at large since then.

Bob Jones: Glory Train

In September 2009, while in a trance, Bob Jones was aboard a train with many other shepherds. Each one had a special seat assigned by the Holy Spirit. Bob asked the Conductor, "What is this train?"

The Conductor told Bob it was the Glory Train and handed him a time capsule that was shaped like an egg. The egg had new life in it! It contained the beginning and end of time. Bob asked the Conductor, "When can I open this egg and when will this train arrive?" The Conductor said the time was within the egg, and the egg will be opened in 2012.

More on the Glory Train

The following are excerpts from an interview recorded with Bob in 2010 about the glory of God leaving the Church in 1977 and its return that is yet to come. This is taken from his videotape and in Bob's language so you can hear his heart and understand what he saw:

"A year ago (2009) I had a vision, and I waited a while to put it all together. And this is the vision I had. The train had come and I boarded it. I had a ticket and a seat. It was a very long train and it didn't have any boxcars on it. It was all just one long large train and you could see from the beginning of the train to the end of it. There were literally thousands of people on this train and they were all sitting down.

"So I found my seat and I sat down too. And, I was wondering where's this train going? What is this train? I saw the Conductor come by so I asked Him, "What is this train?" He said, "This is the Glory Train!" Now I said, "Where are we heading?" He said, "To any city that wants it." And I said, "When will we arrive?" He said, "We will begin to arrive in 2012."

"Then He gave me an egg. And I said, "When do I get to break open this egg?" He said, "in 2012." I said, "What is this egg? What's inside this egg?" He said, "Time."

There was no time before man. Time was created for man. And in this egg there is yesterday's, today's, and tomorrow's time. And every time you hear the train whistle it will remind you of the coming glory." (End of Bob Jones' vision) [ii]

Why Did It Not Happen in 2012?

From Bob's wife Bonnie:

"I believe Bob lived to see the beginning of the billion-soul harvest [revival] and a glimpse of the returning glory. Although it was not the way he expected, the Lord made it possible for Bob to receive his promises in a different way. In the last two years of his life, leaders from around the world came to visit us and would share how Bob's prophetic words impacted the nations.

"Bob had prophesied to some of these leaders twenty-five or thirty-five years ago. These leaders stood on Bob's prophetic word for their ministry as millions of souls were won for the Kingdom. Also, from time to time we would experience the glory in our home. In fact on the day we recorded "The Glory Train" Bob sat in front of the painting in our dining room the artist from Knoxville gifted us. During the message, a brief glimpse of glory came across the painting above Bob's shoulder. It was quick yet definitely visible and caught on video-tape.

"With all my heart, I believe Bob has now received the fullness of God's promise from 1975; the beginning of the billion-soul harvest [revival] and God's returning glory. He now can see the complete picture alongside the Lord. It was not the way Bob expected it to be; it was a million times greater. He can observe the glory as it's released throughout the entire world and have a bird's eye view of the harvest of harvests.

I hope that this encourages you to go higher in the Lord and live daily with greater expectation for the returning glory. Bob, like Caleb, entered into his promises and brought the next generation forward. Now it's up to us to carry forth the torch and ignite the fires." (Bonnie Jones) [iii]

Glory Train Is Coming in 2017

I [Doug Addison] have been tracking the prophetic words of Bob Jones and watching and listening to the Lord for the timing and instructions on how to prepare and fulfill them.

This is why I have been releasing prophetic words for the past few years regarding a revival to the outcasts. In my *2016 Prophetic Forecast* and on my *Spirit Connection* webcast and blog, I go into details about this.

In 2012 I read Bob's prophecy that the Glory Train was coming, but it was evident that something went wrong and the prophecy was never fulfilled. The Lord spoke to me that the train was scheduled to come, but people were too distracted in the United States with the 2012 elections. They were looking for the Lord to return through political parties. Also, there was a misunderstanding that this return was the actual Second Coming of Jesus Christ.

The Lord is not going to return to Earth until we are prepared and there comes a final global harvest and move of God. The *Glory Train prophecy* is coming again and it is about to arrive.

The Lord is saying once again, "Do not be distracted by the political happenings and turmoil being released on the Earth by the enemy." You can be political, but God's return is not going to be in a political party, rather in the hearts of people who desperately need His love.

I contacted Bonnie Jones when I heard this from God. She agreed with me and was hearing the same thing, to not get distracted. God had spoken to me that March 2017 will bring a significant movement towards this. Bonnie said that Bob saw the Glory leave the Church March 17, 1977. So, March 2017 will be the 40-year anniversary of this.

I am a "times and seasons" prophet, and like Bob and many other prophets, we can see things and not fully understand the timing of them. I believe that God is going to do something major in 2017, and it will unfold more over the next few years. Get ready for God's glory to return to the Earth and set us up for one of the biggest revivals in history.

CHAPTER 4

GET READY, REVIVAL IS COMING

"Then the man brought me by way of the north gate to the front of the temple. I looked and saw the glory of the Lord filling the temple of the Lord, and I fell facedown." Ezekiel 44:4

On Christmas morning 2015, I was awakened to an encounter in which I saw a vivid vision of an angel taking measurements for expansion. This angel was very busy and ultra-focused. It reminded me of Ezekiel 40–44 where the angel was measuring to rebuild the temple. Then it became clear that yes, this angel was indeed measuring for a new movement of God coming. This went on for several hours and the angel never spoke a word or even acknowledged me.

Then I saw masses of worker angels assembling to rebuild a spiritual temple because the glory of the Lord is returning like never before. What I was seeing was God preparing for a coming revival. I knew that this "spiritual temple" I was seeing was "The House" that Bob Jones often referred to when he talked about the Billion Soul Revival.

This Christmas encounter was the start of a non-stop flow of revelation that has been steadily increasing. As I said previously, Bob Jones' entire life and ministry was to help us get ready for one of the greatest moves of God and revivals in history. He died in 2014 before it manifested on Earth. But the plans are still in place and God is setting this up right now. There is a lot of shifting happening that is going to bring about a major restructuring for those looking for the next level God has for you in your life.

Bob's Lumberyard Experience

On April 10, 2007, I received a phone call from Bob Jones. He told me about a spiritual experience where he was given a paid receipt from Heaven to buy the lumber to build the "house" for the Billion Soul Revival. In the experience, Bob went into a lumberyard and placed the order from Heaven on the counter, but the foreman refused to fill the order. Bob picked up a silver hammer that was lying there, pounded it on the counter and demanded the goods, but the foreman refused, so Bob left.

Bob told me that the foreman was not a demon, but represented the many leaders and people in the church at that time. He said that the new radical group of outcasts that God wants to draw in is offensive to many Christians.

This new revival that is coming will be raw and messy, but the Church is more comfortable with reaching out to people that seem safer to them.

Bob's health declined after this and he died seven years later in 2014. At that time, many Christians may not have realized that they had said no to this next move of God. Now it is time to pick up the calling and bring it into reality.

Radical Move of God Coming

A week before the Christmas encounter, I heard a distant rumble in the spirit, and it was the Lord coming. The glory of the Lord is returning like never before. It is not coming in the current church structure, though churches are invited.

It will not fit in the old wineskin because it will blow many churches up by causing division. It is because of God's love and mercy for the current Church that He will not allow them or this movement to be damaged.

We will still have our old church structure, and this move of God will be like what happened during the 1950s Healing Revival. That move of God took place mostly outside of churches in tents. I am not saying this new move of God will be tent meetings again, but in a similar fashion, it will happen outside and not inside. In many cases, it will be so big that meetings will need to be in stadiums.

Giant Golden Door Opens

Two months after the Ezekiel 44 Christmas vision, at 4:40 PM, the presence of God came into my car. I had an open vision of a giant golden door that was facing north. It was miles high and wide, and I knew this was a doorway or opportunity coming to us for something new. I knew this vision was connected to the Christmas encounter.

"Then the man brought me by way of the north gate to the front of the temple. I looked and saw the glory of the Lord filling the temple of the Lord, and I fell facedown." Ezekiel 44:4

God spoke to me that the door was something that had never been opened before and it is now being revealed to us.

After that encounter, I started seeing and experiencing the presence and glory of God in greater measure. This spiritual door is still open right now, and God is using it to send revelation and strategies that we will need to enter into this new season.

There Will Be a Cost

Those who say yes to this new movement will pay a great price, but the reward will be even greater. The new anointing of fire and oil from Heaven can only be touched by those who are called by God and have made it through the tests of humility.

This will cause jealousy from many leaders who will try to control or own it—but they will not be able to. This new movement will not be contained by one group and will spread like fire around the world.

All that is happening right now is to set the stage for one of the greatest shows on Earth. Things have already started taking place for a new revival that will become more evident in 2017.

There are pockets of God's glory and fire now being released. There is a lot of repositioning happening, and we can expect to continue to get more clarity on this.

"Come up here, and I will show you what must take place after this." Revelation 4:1b

There are going to be two moves of God. The first will be inside the Church and in the lives of Christians—it is designed to awaken and prepare us.

The second will be a wave of revival that will be geared toward those who have been rejected by Christians, or considered unclean, or even an abomination. What is coming might seem to be a stretch to many people, because some of our current ways of doing things will not work to reach those who have been rejected.

Counsel Meeting in Heaven

On September 22, 2016, I was awakened at 2:30 AM, and the Holy Spirit said "Get up, because an important Counsel meeting has taken place." In the spirit I saw members of the Counsel of Heaven; I heard the late prophet, Bob Jones, speaking to them.

As I mentioned, Bob was on Earth to release a great revival that would reach over one billion people, people who would be a radical group for God. This never took place before his death in 2014, but God has not forgotten Bob's life and ministry. It is now time for this revival to start.

In the Counsel of Heaven, the Lord was making plans for this new movement. I saw transitional teams of angels being dispersed. Assignments were being given to people who will be part of this new move of God. There will not be only one person who will lead it. I saw the *hidden ones* starting to awaken. These are the ones who, like Joseph in Genesis 41, had been hidden in prison, then came on the scene and changed the course of history through the prophetic gifts and dream interpretation.

Calling All Outcasts

The rest of this chapter is an excerpt from my *2016 Prophetic Forecast* book. It is relevant and will help bring clarity to what God is doing now.

"Then He [Jesus] *said to them, 'The harvest truly is great, but the laborers are few; therefore pray the Lord of the harvest to send out laborers into His harvest.'"* Luke 10:2 NKJV

I do not know a better way to describe the people that God is moving on right now. God spoke to me that this group is the spiritual outcasts because many of them have suffered rejection and wounding from Christians who have not understood them. There has been a lot of relational fallout with those outside of Christianity. This is sad because the people who need God the most have been rejected because of their beliefs or lifestyles.

In my experience many spiritual outcasts actually do not have anything against God. But most of them have something negative to say about God's people. This is very sad and if you are reading this book and you are one of the people who have been wounded or rejected, I would like to say, "I am sorry for all that happened to you and ask for your forgiveness."

The Parable of the Great Banquet

The Parable of the Great Banquet is a prophetic word for now. In Luke 14:15–24, Jesus told a parable of the Great Banquet in which a man was putting on a big feast and invited everyone to come. But they all made excuses and were too busy. So the man sent his servants out to invite the outcasts.

"At the time of the banquet he sent his servant to tell those who had been invited, 'Come, for everything is now ready.'"
Luke 14:17

Because the ones who were invited got busy and did not come, the Master had to invite other people.

"Go out quickly into the streets and alleys of the town and bring in the poor, the crippled, the blind and the lame."
Luke 14:21b

This is a prophetic word from God right now: "Come, for everything is ready." God has prepared an opportunity for us and we are being given an invitation to be part of something big that God has been planning.

This represents the spiritual outcasts that God is drawing in now. This next move of God is similar to this parable. Many have been invited to be part of it but have gotten caught up in other things that are not in God's timing or His heart.

God's heart is for all people to come into the banquet. He is going to let the spiritually poor, crippled, blind, and lame be part of it. The spiritual homeless are being invited to the party. These are the ones who have been rejected by Christians and the Church.

God spoke to me that we need to understand this parable and not be too busy or distracted or we will miss the invitation at hand. God's agenda is to love people and bring healing. This includes the prodigal sons and daughters, pastors' kids, those who grew up going to church and many who are offended by or dislike Christianity.

These are the ones who are into strange things and unusual lifestyles that you might not agree with. Does this sound familiar? Many of these are our own children and grandchildren. God has been saving them for a new movement that they are called to be part of. He has not allowed them to come into the Kingdom too early because you cannot pour new wine into old wineskins or it will make a mess of things.

[Jesus said] *"Neither do people pour new wine into old wineskins. If they do, the skins will burst; the wine will run out and the wineskins will be ruined. No, they pour new wine into new wineskins, and both are preserved."* Matthew 9:17

Note that Jesus said, so that *"both are preserved."* God values the old ways and the new. He is not going to suddenly annihilate the old ways of doing things. However, God is making this new movement a priority right now. He will be shifting favor and finances to "new wine and wineskin" efforts.

God has been saving them for a new movement that they are called to be part of. We are about to see a move of God come to these groups.

Like many movements and revivals in the past, many Christians will be tempted to judge it as not being from God. Pray that God opens our eyes to what He is doing and gives us His heart for people!

Healing of Spiritual Leprosy

In Jesus' day, there were plenty of spiritual outcasts. One big group was people with leprosy that were considered unclean and banned from worshiping God. Yet Jesus focused a lot of His time ministering to this group. Today we have our share of perceived "spiritual lepers." These untouchable, unlovable groups are all around us crying out for someone to get real with them like Jesus did.

I am not saying the people groups I am about to mention are bad people or spiritual lepers. I mean that many Christians view them this way.

They are Democrats (or any political party other than our own), people involved in abortion, the tattooed or pierced, New Age, and LGBT (gay and lesbian), to name just a few. God loves people unconditionally. We must heal the gap between the Church and the spiritual outcasts.

God is releasing a new anointing of power and love for those who have been unloved and unwanted by the Church. God's new agenda is to heal those who have been wounded by Christianity. Their cries for justice have reached the ears of the Lord and this is why the next move of God will be focused on the spiritual outcasts.

No Longer an Abomination

Even though Jesus instructed the disciples to take His message and power to all people, they got hung up on certain people groups. Spiritual pride and prejudice set in and it took a major spiritual encounter to heal this and ignite a new movement once again.

In the time of the early Church, the Jewish people still considered many Gentiles (non-Jewish people) to be an abomination when it came to the foods they ate and some of their practices. This caused division and it prevented the Gentiles from experiencing the fullness of God. In Galatians 2 the apostle Paul corrects Peter on his prideful and prejudiced behavior.

In Acts 10, Peter had a supernatural encounter in a vision where God spoke to him to not call anything unclean that He had made clean. We need to be careful that we do not fall into the same trap that holds people back from experiencing God's love.

God is moving on a group of spiritual outcasts and He is making them clean through His love and grace. Yes, this is a radical message and it will look very messy, just as it did in the early Church. Those that are currently called an abomination by Christians are going to be made clean by God.[iv]

CHAPTER 5

WEAK SHEEP DEFENDERS

"Behold my servant, whom I uphold, my chosen, in whom my soul delights; I have put my Spirit upon him; he will bring forth justice to the nations. He will not cry aloud or lift up his voice, or make it heard in the street; a bruised reed he will not break, and a faintly burning wick he will not quench; he will faithfully bring forth justice." Isaiah 42:1-3 ESV

There is a new sound being broadcast from Heaven right now. It is coming to the pulpits, the airways, the music, the news ... and to anyone that has ears to hear. This is new revelation of God's love and justice that will bring healing to those who were wounded or oppressed. God is releasing those who were bound by the judgments of others and those who have had great callings, but were held down by a spirit of pride and prejudice.

We are going to continue to see injustices revealed. God is revealing the deeds of those who have wounded people and broken their spirits.

A new Spirit of Justice is ringing out. Those that have nearly lost their light and way will suddenly come back to life.

Signs in the Super Bowl 2013

On Sunday, February 3, 2013, my *Daily Prophetic Word* was, "A Prophetic Sign from God will be seen around the world." During the third quarter of the Super Bowl game between the Baltimore Ravens and the San Francisco 49ers, half of the lights went out for 34 minutes in the New Orleans Superdome. God spoke to me that this was a prophetic sign out of Ezekiel 34.

- When the lights went out, the score of the game was 28-6; and 28 plus 6 equals 34.
- The lights were out for 34 minutes total.
- The power outage happened in the third quarter (3 of 4 or 3/4).
- The winning team's final score was 34.
- Ezekiel 34 ends with verse 31.
- The exact Super Bowl ending score was 34–31.

The old generators at the Superdome caused half of the lights to go out. This is a prophetic sign that the old ways of doing things will not produce the full power we need right now to be a light to the world. Even the fact that the Super Bowl was in New Orleans, and it involved teams like San Francisco and Baltimore (East Coast and West Coast) shows us that God is going to move in places that we least expect.

There are many prophetic signs in Ezekiel 34 about what God is going to do.

Ezekiel 34 Mantles

On June 9, 2016, I had a radical encounter. I was suddenly standing in the Courts of Heaven and a Counsel meeting was taking place (similar to Zechariah 3). God spoke to me with a thundering voice, "Son, prophesy Ezekiel 34!" I knew the meaning of Ezekiel 34 because God had spoken it to me previously with the prophecy I had released in February 2013, *Super Bowl: Prophetic Sign Seen by the World.*

In the encounter, I was shown parts of Ezekiel 34 that are now God's agenda for those who have been wounded by mean shepherds and fat sheep. These wounded, weak sheep are people who need God's love and have been driven away from churches. It goes on to say that the mean shepherds and fat sheep who do not have God's heart of love are allowing the enemy to ravish the weaker sheep.

I have been bringing a similar prophetic word for many years. One of the next revivals is going to be in this group of spiritual outcasts that have been rejected and considered unclean by many Christians. This may include women stepping up into leadership, political parties that are not accepted by many Christians, those with tattoos and piercings, the ones who are into zombies and vampires, New Age people, LGBT and minorities, to name a few.

We do not have to agree with the things people might believe and support. God is calling us to love them unconditionally. I am not saying they are unclean, but they have been rejected and mistreated terribly by some Christians over the years. They have been looked upon by Christians as unclean, but God is about to do some amazing miracles in these groups of people.

Many have been scattered and driven away from the opportunity to worship Jesus. As an evangelist and missionary to the outcasts for years, I have heard countless horror stories of the damage and rejection they have received "in the Name of Jesus." Many Christians have driven people away from God.

"You have not strengthened the weak or healed the sick or bound up the injured. You have not brought back the strays or searched for the lost. You have ruled them harshly

and brutally. So they were scattered because there was no shepherd, and when they were scattered they became food for all the wild animals." Ezekiel 34:4–5

"Therefore this is what the Sovereign Lord says to them: See, I myself will judge between the fat sheep and the lean sheep. Because you shove with flank and shoulder, butting all the weak sheep with your horns until you have driven them away, I will save my flock, and they will no longer be plundered. I will judge between one sheep and another." Ezekiel 34:20–22

God Is Looking for People to Show Love

God is the judge of each person's heart and motives. This is a time to step up and be a light in darkness.

We really can love people who have been wounded by religion and by Christians who do not love as Jesus does. This is an injustice in the eyes of God, and He is preparing a movement to gather them to a safe place.

"I will establish one shepherd over them, and he shall feed them—My servant David. He shall feed them and be their shepherd. And I, the Lord, will be their God, and My servant David a prince among them; I, the Lord, have spoken." Ezekiel 34:23–24 NKJV

David is symbolic of someone who loves God and will be a warrior to protect and draw the outcasts to God (David's mighty men were outcasts, 1 Samuel 22:2). This is a time when we need to have a heart like David for people who have been wounded and driven away from having a relationship with God.

Weak Sheep Defender Mantles

While I was in the Courts of Heaven prophesying this, I felt a mantle come on me and the heat of it has not lifted.

I heard the Lord say to deputize *Weak Sheep Defenders.* God's heart and agenda right now is to raise up people who are willing to go after those who were driven away, be defenders of the weak and menders of those who were driven away. A strong ministry of reconciliation is coming on those who are willing to step up and receive it.

I have been prophesying this and doing outreaches for many years. One of the reasons I got very sick for a few years was because I was being cursed by Christians for doing what Jesus would have done and because I was reaching into the groups I mentioned above.

I encourage you to read Ezekiel 34 for yourself. I am not focusing on the judgment of the mean shepherds and the fat sheep because God is more interested in helping those who are hurting.

We need to become Holy Spirit MASH units (Mobile Army Surgical Hospitals) to the weak and the outcasts.

New Ways to Operate

God is revealing new strategic ways to operate so that we can be more effective in our changing times. Here are a few things you can do now:

- Break through religiosity, which means acting too religious to connect with people.

- Love people unconditionally, like Jesus did. You do not have to agree with people to love them. Being kind in the face of disagreement is a start.

- Separate religion from politics. God's heart is for people, not political parties. You can indeed be politically active, but we cannot justify hatred toward people as "hating what they represent."

- Allow people time to experience God. Sometimes requiring them to change too quickly will do more harm than good.

Love Overcomes

Jesus said in John 16:8 that the Holy Spirit will come and convict the world of guilt in regard to sin. God's task is to convict people of sin, and ours is to love people.

"*... Love your neighbor as yourself.*" Matthew 22:39b

When we do love people unconditionally, showing love to one another, then people will know that we are true followers of Jesus.

"A new command I give you: Love one another. As I have loved you, so you must love one another. By this everyone will know that you are my disciples, if you love one another." John 13:34–35

I realize that this may be a difficult prophetic word for some people, but we are living in difficult times. I am doing my best to present what I heard from God without sounding judgmental myself to those who are inadvertently mistreating people. My hope and prayer is that we can all love one another without judging. Love conquers all!

Prophesy over Dry Bones

Many of those who are called to be part of these new movements have been discouraged and in the *dark night of the soul,* or wilderness. I heard the Lord say to prophesy Ezekiel 37, (a call to the Valley of Dry Bones) and to awaken those who will have ears to hear.

I began to prophesy this over people during this encounter:

"Then He said to me, 'Prophesy to these bones and say to them, "Dry bones, hear the word of the Lord! ... I will make breath enter you, and you will come to life."'

" ... Then he said to me, "Prophesy to the breath ... 'This is what the Sovereign Lord says: Come, breath, from four winds and breath into these slain, that they may live.'" Ezekiel 37:4–9

Then the Lord spoke to me, and said:

"I, the Lord, am breathing new life into you so that you can raise up the army that is coming forward in 2017. For this reason, I am going to move fast and I am going to move furiously in your life. I am going to pour out My fire and glory upon you. I am going to realign you into a place of effectiveness."

CHAPTER 6

ANGELS AND KEYS TO THE KINGDOM

"Are not all angels ministering spirits sent to serve those who will inherit salvation?" Hebrews 1:14

Expect to have greater angelic encounters this year. God is releasing and activating angels around us in greater measure. Because darkness is increasing in the world, God is sending us ministering angels to help us personally and to prepare for a great revival that is coming.

Angels have various purposes and assignments. Some are around us all the time, while others are waiting to be activated for one sole purpose. It is important to understand that you do not have to see an angel to have an encounter.

I have angelic encounters often. Sometimes I see them, but most of the time I just know they are there.

Angels normally do not show themselves because they do not want to distract from their assignment or what they are bringing to us. You will see this in Revelation 19:10. When John saw an angel and felt the glory of God, he was tempted to worship the angel. For this reason, angels are normally cloaked (hidden) from us.

In Acts 10, Cornelius saw an angel distinctly. In Acts 12, Peter had an encounter with an angel that broke him out of prison. He did not know if it was a vision, or if the angel was real. For me it is the same way. Sometimes I do not know if I am just having a vision or if I am actually experiencing the events.

What matters most is that we are able to receive from the Lord what the angel is bringing to us, whether it is a plan, revelation, encouragement or the ability to overcome a situation.

The Gathering Angels

Eight years ago in 2009, I had several radical encounters with angels in Cape Town, South Africa. I was taken in real time in the Spirit back to the United States and I saw groups of specially designed and assigned angels, called Gathering Angels. These angels are mentioned by Jesus in Mark 13:27.

That night, I was in my hotel room in South Africa. I lay down on the bed, and I was suddenly back in California driving down Highway 101 heading south. I was trying to figure out if this was really happening to me, or if I was dreaming, or if it was a vision—but it felt completely real!

As I was driving, I realized God had "transported" me. And I looked over and there were Department of Transportation workers on the side of the road. They were all bent over at an angle, scooping things up and putting them into bags. There were about twelve workers, and they all turned their heads at the same time and locked eyes with me.

In that moment, their faces turned into angelic faces with red eyes that looked like laser beams, and the fear of God hit me. The Lord spoke to me that they were the *Gathering Angels*. They have only one assignment and purpose—that is for evangelism and revival. They get activated and go to work helping with the harvest of souls during revival time. Then they go back into waiting mode.

They all went back to work. Their faces turned back down, and I could see that they were scooping balls of white light into bags. The Holy Spirit spoke to me that these Gathering Angels are being sent around the world right now to prepare us for revival.

"And he will send his angels and gather his elect from the four winds, from the ends of the earth to the ends of the heavens." Mark 13:27

The balls of white light they were gathering at the side of the freeway were the souls of people. I was told these were people that had been discarded, overlooked or wounded by the Church. These Gathering Angels had come to scoop them up to be used by God.

I came back into my body, and I was sweating and shaking. God spoke to me, and said that He is sending squads of Gathering Angels all over the Earth to prepare for a global harvest. The people He is coming for are those who have been considered outcasts and have been discarded by the Church and wounded by Christianity. In Mark 13:27 they operate in the *four winds,* which means they can move in power and blow things into place quickly.

Where Are They Now?

From 2009 and over the next few years, I saw them in various places around the world. Every time I would see a squad of them, they were not activated to their fullest extent but were in waiting mode. They are waiting for their assignments to be activated.

This was eight years ago, and God spoke to me that as His glory returns to the Church it will activate the Gathering Angels.

I saw a group stationed in Hamilton, Ontario, Canada in 2015. I prophesied that a movement of God would come to Hamilton one year later in May 2016.

Sure enough, Todd Bentley and Fresh Fire USA began doing extended meetings there in May 2016, and a healing revival broke out. The Gathering Angels are all over the Earth now and are being positioned to prepare us to gather in the outcasts.

Keys to the Kingdom

God is also releasing new keys of authority. He is shifting the holders of these keys and mantles from the ones who were not using them, into the hands of those who will.

"I will give you the keys of the kingdom of heaven; whatever you bind on earth will be bound in heaven, and whatever you loose on earth will be loosed in heaven." Matthew 16:19

Jesus gave Peter the keys of the Kingdom of Heaven, which is the authority that can open and close things in the spiritual realm. God is releasing new revelation this year on keys and principles of the Kingdom. There is greater understanding coming on how to use our authority that is given to us by Jesus.

In some cases, spiritual authority has been used to control people and not set them free. Jesus proclaimed His purpose and calling on Earth in Luke 4:18b:

"*... He has sent me to proclaim freedom for the prisoners and recovery of sight for the blind, to set the oppressed free ...*"

Our call from the Lord is to set people free and not bind them up with rules or try to control people for our own purposes or programs.

Keys of Authority Reassigned

I originally released this prophetic word on my blog in 2016, but this is something that is not limited to time. God is continuing to do this all around the Earth, particularly around the first of each year. There are spiritual keys that have been given to people that unlock and lock things in the spiritual realm in and over people and regions.

This is similar to the key of David mentioned in Revelation 3:7b:

"... These are the words of him who is holy and true, who holds the key of David. What he opens no one can shut, and what he shuts no one can open."

There is also a key of David mentioned in Isaiah 22:22. This is in the Old Testament, and is mentioned in the context of judgment. But the key in Revelation 3:7 is the redeemed key of authority that can open and close things with God's heart and love.

There are people with spiritual authority operating in the Old Testament version of this gift. They often close things down in their anger and opinions (Isaiah 22:22). Their actions have caused so much pain to so many people that God has begun to reassign the keys to others.

On several occasions, I have seen angels traveling the world gathering these keys, gifts and assignments. This is happening over ministries, churches, businesses, cities and even nations. God is reassigning these specific keys of authority to those who are humble and hungry to see God move to set the captives free. Some of these reassignments were at a major level over a city or a region. Others were gifts being reassigned to do the work of the Lord at varying levels.

Apostolic Keys over Cities

Some apostolic leaders who carried keys of authority over cities or regions had laid down their callings or, in some cases, had gotten bitter and judgmental. This caused God's greater purposes for these areas to be put on hold or get sidetracked.

I saw several cities that were high in immorality and crime, and the world looks at them through the eyes of judgment. The condition of these cities was actually the result of the person carrying the apostolic key who had gotten judgmental or laid it down.

God is reassigning these apostolic keys and callings to new leaders that will fulfill the purposes of Heaven. In many cases, it will not be given to a single person but to several. The new apostles will not see their calling as a title, but as a function and assignment in the Kingdom of God.

Many of these new leaders will appear to be the least likely because they have been under the radar and humble. But they will start to emerge, and we will see outpourings of God's power and mercy that will get the attention of the world.

Key Angel Dream

I had a prophetic dream that I was with another prophet, and we needed to get a key duplicated. We found a special key store that was on a mountain. The doors of the key store were locked.

I peered through the store's tiny window and saw a special key duplication machine inside. I felt an urgency from the Lord to get in at all costs, so I broke the glass and opened the door.

I was greeted by an angel who handed me two blank keys. One of them was an ancient-looking key that was tarnished, and the other was bright and rainbow-colored. This angel was the only one who could operate the key machine.

As we walked towards the machine, a rattlesnake appeared between me and the angel, and suddenly it lunged out towards me. I caught it in midair and strangled it. That was the end of the dream.

God is giving keys to us in this new season. The tiny window to the key shop represents having too small of a vision. In order to break through to something new, we will need to break through limitations and sometimes go against what we might normally think is the right thing to do.

The rattlesnake is a demonic attack trying to "rattle us" and get us distracted from getting the new keys for new connections that God is bringing.

The blank keys represent God bringing things to us. The ancient key represents gifts and callings from the past that have been reserved for this time. The rainbow-colored key, which represents new covenantal promises from God, has specifically been reserved for this time in history. God is bringing out the old and the new that will open new doors of opportunity to us.

This is a powerful symbol of God's intentions for us right now as God is assigning keys of authority. We will need to ascend the mountain of the Lord and break through attacks and limitations to get them. This year we can expect to see new opportunities, gifts and callings emerge. We will need to battle to get them.

A Key from a Prophet

During the time that I got this revelation, I also had a dramatic spiritual experience. During the early morning hours, while lying in bed, I had a vision. An angel walked into my bedroom and handed me a tarnished key and told me it had belonged to a major prophet who was no longer using it. It was called the Key of Light, and it could open life over people. It could also close things down over a person or situation as well. I was told that the prophet who had previously held this key had gotten judgmental and began using it to close things down more than open things up.

I noticed that my authority in the spirit began to increase after this. I was able to see the plans of the Lord more clearly and also the plans of the enemy. I began to use this new key of authority to open up God's intentions for people, cities and nations.

I could also close off the plans of the enemy. As we get rid of judgments and get God's heart of love and blessings, then He can trust us with new gifts and authority.

How to Respond

"For all those who exalt themselves will be humbled, and those who humble themselves will be exalted." Luke 14:11

We can ask God to give us new gifts, but ultimately it is God who assigns these new keys of authority and apostolic callings. Watch for new gifts and authority to come to you in a greater measure this year.

You do not have to have a dramatic experience like I am describing to receive new keys of authority. God will bring this to you at the level of maturity that you can currently handle. This is not about having a spiritual experience or seeing an angel. It is about taking what God gives you by faith and running with it.

Getting healed of being judgmental will open the doors for these new gifts to flow through you. God is looking for people He can trust because this next movement will involve having the character of Jesus' love and grace.

Being humble and allowing the Lord to take away things that are not of the Kingdom is a necessity. Promotions and advancements will come as you go through a John 15 pruning experience.

There are beliefs, doctrines and ways of operating that are no longer working or beneficial in this new season. God is pruning us all right now. This means that He is pointing out and removing things that are not needed.

What will remain are only things that are of God's Kingdom for this particular time and season. Although this might include sin, it is primarily beliefs and doctrines that are not for now.

John 15 Pruning

"I am the true vine, and my Father is the gardener. He cuts off every branch in me that bears no fruit, while every branch that does bear fruit he prunes so that it will be even more fruitful. You are already clean because of the word I have spoken to you. Remain in me, as I also remain in you. No branch can bear fruit by itself; it must remain in the vine. Neither can you bear fruit unless you remain in me." John 15:1–4

This time of deeper cleansing will result in a closer relationship with God, and you will have greater authority.

"If you remain in me and my words remain in you, ask whatever you wish, and it will be done for you." John 15:7

God's desire for us is to have joy, love and unity. He is healing those who have been operating in the opposite of these qualities.

"I have told you this so that my joy may be in you and that your joy may be complete. My command is this: Love each other as I have loved you." John 15:11–12

Love is the key to all that we do. This is an overlooked commandment, but God is calling us back to the simplicity of loving like Jesus did. This means to love people that are different than us. This is part of the stretching that is coming.

"You did not choose me, but I chose you and appointed you so that you might go and bear fruit—fruit that will last—and so that whatever you ask in my name the Father will give you. This is my command: Love each other." John 15:16–17

You are being called and chosen to bear the fruit of the Spirit (Galatians 5:22–23), and to help others. Love is what will get us through this new season. If you have been operating on fumes, then it is time to refuel with love and joy.

CHAPTER 7

RELEASED FROM HOUSE ARREST

On several occasions and in various places I go, I have been shown that many people were experiencing limitations in the Kingdom or House of God. It was as if they had been placed under *house arrest.*

When someone is placed under house arrest, generally they are not allowed to leave their place of residence. Instead of going to jail, they are a prisoner in their own home and have to wear an ankle monitor. Spiritually, many have felt that they are under house arrest within the House of God. God is releasing people from this condition, and He is going to change their house arrest into a house of rest.

There are seasons we all go through in which it seems like we are not being acknowledged or released into our fullest potential. God uses these times to train and develop foundational character in us. Sometimes this can feel like house arrest. The best way to get through these trying seasons is to rest in the fact that God has your best interest in mind. But God says that all things are becoming new.

"He who was sitting on the throne said, 'I am making everything new!' Then he said, 'Write this down. You can trust these words. They are true.'" Revelation 21:5 NIRV

God wants you to keep trusting Him and know that His prophetic promises and words are true. You are free from the chains that have kept you in a place of confinement and restriction. Your freedom, a new freedom, is yours! Difficult times, being misunderstood and betrayed are being cut off from you. Instead of house arrest, God is giving you a place of peace. God is changing your house arrest into a house of rest. We are entering into a new season of freedom, peace and rest.

Notice that many people in the Bible went through seasons of their lives that were limiting, including Moses, Joseph, David, Paul and Peter to name a few. God used these times to develop them for later accomplishments.

I went through several seasons in which I felt like I was under house arrest. Years later, I now see how I needed those seasons to develop my character, and I am now learning how to enter into God's rest. My prayer for you is that you will find new freedom and peace even as you read these words.

There are many people who have been in a time of limitations. As a result, they are now in solitary confinement. God is calling those who have been in isolation to come out. Many of you were wounded and rejected, and you recoiled. It is time to come out and experience a new level of healing and restoration.

Releasing What Was Bound

Sometimes it is God who is causing limitations in our lives. Other times it can be that judgments spoken against us by others, even leaders, are holding us back. There are judgments that have been made by Christians that may also need to be released.

This year it is important to get set free from these so you can fulfill what God is calling you to. Judgments against others cause us to come into agreement with darkness and not with the Lord. A name for Satan in the Bible is the accuser of the believers. We do not want to come into agreement with that. We need to agree with Heaven over a person, city and nation.

"'Truly I tell you, whatever you bind on earth will be bound in heaven, and whatever you loose on earth will be

loosed in heaven. Again, truly I tell you that if two of you on earth agree about anything they ask for, it will be done for them by my Father in heaven.'" Matthew 18:18–19

There are times when leaders or mentors can hold us back from advancing. This may or may not be intentional on their part. Sometimes it is from the spirit of fear or jealousy. Other times they really like what you are bringing to them, and they want to utilize your gifts and abilities to help their ministries. This is not always bad, but if you are feeling stuck and limited, then it might be time to get set free.

Jesus talks about when we bind things on Earth then they are bound in Heaven (Matthew 18:18–19). This applies to people as well as spiritual matters. We can pass judgment or use our authority to limit a person on Earth.

As a result, we are limiting them spiritually (in Heaven). This prophetic word might not be for everyone, but there are those who are being called to the next level and you are being held back by people and leaders.

Many of you who are called to more have a spirit of honor and loyalty, and because of that, you may have a built-in habit of staying too long or not feeling released to go. We do need to wait on God's timing to make major changes. If you are not feeling released and you are in a stagnant, dead place, then this might be for you. It is time to move to a place of life.

Stuck in the Past

It is time now to set people free from these past connections. This might not be for everyone. But if you have felt stuck in the past, or you were once part of a group, and are no longer with them—then it is possible this is for you.

For many of us, we experienced heavenly access to revelation for the first time through various pastors, apostolic and prophetic leaders, or other ministries we felt connected to. And they opened things up for us based on their anointing.

A biblical example of this is what Jesus said to Nathanael in John 1:50–51. He told Nathanael that he would see Heaven open and angels ascending and descending upon Him [Jesus]. This indicates that we could get an open Heaven of revelation and understanding by being around certain teachers and leaders.

Sometimes God changes the season of our life. Through this process, He is bringing new revelation; yet our spirit might still be stuck in the previous time. I am not talking about changing the message of Jesus or distorting it to fit our needs. I am referring to when God legitimately moves us to a new time, and the old ways of doing things are no longer as effective as they were before.

Two Examples of This

In Matthew 9:14–17, the Pharisees and some of John the Baptist's followers asked Jesus why He did not do the things they did, such as fast. They were stuck in the past and were not able to recognize the new thing God was doing.

In Acts 19:1–7, the apostle Paul met a group of Christians who had only received the baptism of John the Baptist, and did not know the full message of Jesus and the infilling of the Holy Spirit. They were stuck in the past because they had not gotten the new revelation of Jesus yet.

If you have felt adrift or disconnected and you are not sure why, or you have recently changed affiliations—this might be for you.

Released from Saul

God is gathering a remnant of warriors, similar to David's mighty men and women, to cross over into this new season. Like David, before he could move into his new season he was pursued by King Saul. David and Saul both were given a prophetic word by the prophet Samuel to be King. Saul was the current King, who had lost God's heart for people. David was the up-and-coming new movement that was not fully released yet.

It is common for leaders of previous moves of God to not understand the new. This happened throughout the Bible. It is important for us to use David as a model for how to deal with these seasons of our life. David honored Saul even though Saul was pursuing him to take his life. David waited on God in the midst of this time of testing.

This happened to Jesus as well. When He came on the scene, the current spiritual leaders became jealous and tried to take His life. It happened to the apostle Paul as well, and it is happening to many people today.

If you are called to be part of the new movement of God, then there is a chance that you have a Saul who does not understand you and might even be pursuing you. The principle of binding on Earth and in Heaven, which we just discussed, plays a part in this.

David was a man of love and justice for the people. God is raising up a new movement who will have a new heart like David—who was for God and the people. God is birthing a new movement on Earth that is now starting.

To be part of it, you will need to get set free from the rule of "the Sauls" in your life. You will need to take action to get out of the tough places and the dead or stagnant past seasons.

Spirit of Honor

I realize this could be a dangerous prophetic word. There are people who need to go through these seasons of limitations, and God uses the dark nights of our soul to train us.

He will allow us to serve under a Saul, or difficult leader, to develop us. Jesus operated His ministry during the heavy rule of the Pharisees and teachers of the Law. He encouraged His disciples to honor those in positions of leadership while not doing the things they did.

"The teachers of the law and the Pharisees sit in Moses' seat. So you must be careful to do everything they tell you. But do not do what they do, for they do not practice what they preach." Matthew 23:2–3

If you feel these prophetic words are for you, then I encourage you to honor the leaders God has placed in your life the best you can. If you are in a dead place or one that is spiritually abusive, then it is time to move into a place where you are celebrated and not just tolerated.

Just so you know, not all leaders are going to agree or honor you in your process. What is important is that you obey the Lord and use love and integrity in all you do.

CHAPTER 8

FIXING THE NET

"'Yes indeed, it won't be long now.' God's Decree. 'Things are going to happen so fast your head will swim, one thing fast on the heels of the other. You won't be able to keep up. Everything will be happening at once—and everywhere you look, blessings! Blessings like wine pouring off the mountains and hills.'" Amos 9:13 MSG

Bullet Train Arrived

Get ready for things to happen fast. In the midst of some very heavy trials and storms, the Lord did some things suddenly. On October 19, while praying, I had a vision of a bullet train arriving. The Lord announced to those who are ready for the ride of their life to get aboard. Things are already starting to accelerate as we are moving into a time of seeing sudden changes and sudden advancement.

Things are now going to move way more quickly to restore you into a new place. God is equipping us with new weapons for our spiritual warfare. He is releasing new gifts and anointing that are updated from the old, and they are much more effective. He is releasing strategies that will open up worldwide evangelism and He is releasing financial strategies for us to accomplish this big calling.

The Net 2011 by Bob Jones

Bob Jones released a prophetic article on his website in 2011 that is significant and similar to what God is doing right now.

From Bob:

"In a vision I saw a fishing net and it was completely full of large fish. The net had a hole in it and the fish escaped. Then I was shown a tool that would be used to mend the net. It was a special type of tool that the Lord was giving to some of His approved leaders of the church. This tool was for networking!

"If you're going to be part of the harvest, several churches will need to come together; laying down their private agenda and surrender to God's eternal purpose. One church will not be able to hold all the fish.

"It will take several that network together who allow the Holy Spirit to lead them into one of the greatest harvest we have ever seen.

"I believe this vision is Peter's net. The 153 fish in Peter's net represent the nations of the world …

"This net is for the nations. It is time we ask the Lord to give us the nations!

… We will need to be joined together in spirit, not in mind or soul. We will need to become servants to the Holy Spirit to pull this net in." (End of Bob Jones' Vision)[v]

Fixing the Net

The Internet was created by God to bring Him glory. It is evident that the enemy is trying to inflict fear and use it for the wrong reasons. 2017 will be the start of taking back the Internet for God's glory and to bring the message of the gospel to the nations. With the rise of smartphones, people in the poorest and most remote places might not have a computer, but they have access to the Internet through their phones.

I want to share with you something I went through over the past few years because it is relevant to what is happening now. After the 2008 economic downturn, it became more difficult for ministries and churches to travel and impact the world as we once had.

In the midst of this, God gave me a new strategy for ministry, but I was having trouble transitioning into it. I had an emotional tie to the past that was preventing me from moving into the future. We started experiencing a lot of warfare, and began to lose money. I was exhausted.

Then, before he went to Heaven, Bob Jones called me and shared a vision God had given him about me. Bob saw all kinds of computers that were all connected together with wires. He was seeing the Internet, but he did not have words for it. The enemy was using these computers and the wires for evil. Then an angel gave me a silver hacksaw. I began cutting into the wires and short-circuiting the plans of the enemy and put in the glory of God instead.

God Wants to Use the Internet

I have a high-technology background, and I did my best to activate this prophetic word by launching our first *Spirit Connection* webcasts in 2008. It was a terrible year for us. We went through a major split within our ministry, I stopped getting speaking invitations, and our website got hacked. On top of it we went $30,000 in debt.

In spite of all the warfare, I stayed with the ministry God had called me to do through the Internet. But I was still giving 90% of my time and energy to traveling to live conferences too. I had almost given up on the vision until 2012, when God gave me a radical new strategy. We were able to pay off the $30,000 of debt in a matter of three days. It took a major mindset change for me to do ministry in a different way.

Today we are debt-free. We have an Internet-based ministry with 95% of our staff being virtual workers. My *Daily Prophetic Words*, monthly *Spirit Connection* webcast and blog now go all over the world. We are able to touch way more people than we would have, had I stayed with our old strategy. But I had to let go of the past to get into the future.

I now have the freedom to go where God calls me to go, when He calls me to. As you let go of the past, you will make room for God to give you a new strategy.

Radio, TV and the Internet

In the early 1920s, healing evangelist Aimee Semple McPherson rocked the entire world with God's love and power. She was one of the few people who was able to radically change the arts and entertainment industry in Hollywood, California. She also used the cutting-edge media of radio. She owned one of the first Christian radio stations and broadcast her messages in a new way.

Similarly, God gave Rex Humbard, a pastor in Akron, Ohio, a vision to take the message of Jesus into the homes of people all over the world through television. He started the first Christian television network in the 1950s. Humbard influenced so many people in the entertainment industry with his willingness to use media that he was asked to officiate Elvis Presley's funeral.

The next move of God will utilize the Internet. This is why Satan is trying to terrorize people and scare them from using it. The Internet was created by God and not Satan. It was intended to bring about a great move that is indeed coming.

Jesus and the Internet

Just as radio and television were used in the past, God is bringing a new calling and anointing to the Internet. In Luke 5, Jesus actually did something similar—He stood in a boat to broadcast His message to more people. Previously, speakers were limited to buildings and synagogues. But Jesus used a method of communicating that made it easy for the common people to hear and understand Him.

Then Jesus turned to the owners of the boat and said, "Put out to deep water." He was going to show these seasoned fishermen how to fish in a new way. He showed them supernaturally where the fish were located. When they let down their nets, there were so many fish that the nets broke.

God is releasing a new strategy to use the Internet for something different than it is currently being used for. He is calling us to "fix the net" (Internet). There are angels and heavenly resources being released right now to repair the damage from the Internet and bring us new strategies to "catch fish" for the Kingdom. This is symbolic of encountering people in need of God's love.

Peter's Net

In Luke 5, when Jesus entered Peter's boat, He instructed them where to let down their nets. They caught so many fish that their nets broke. They had to signal for help from another boat, and together they caught so many fish that both boats nearly sank.

Fishing is a prophetic sign of evangelism, the Kingdom of God and doing God's will. Indeed, the early Church in the Book of Acts experienced this as many began to follow them.

To the disciples, this was the equivalent of being in deep water. They were stretched as God opened salvation to people groups that were outside their comforts or beliefs (Acts 10).

Luke 5 was a prophetic parable of what Jesus is now calling us to. But there was also another fishing encounter that Peter and a few disciples had with Jesus in John 21.

During a time when things looked discouraging, Jesus stood on the shore and called out to them to let down their nets. But this time He told them to cast the nets on the other side of the boat. Again, they caught a large number of fish, but this time the nets did not break.

The prophetic message in the John 21 experience is that they had to cast their nets on the opposite side of the boat. God is drawing people, but they are not where we might think. This is what God is calling us to in the new revival that is coming. The "fish" are in deep water and in different places than we might think.

Also in John 21, Peter had previously denied the Lord three times, and felt like he had messed up. But in this encounter Peter was restored to his Kingdom calling. Many people who have felt that they either messed up or have been hidden or forgotten are suddenly going to have an encounter with the Lord and be restored to fulfill the reason they were created.

We Will Need a Kingdom Mindset

Just as in Luke 5, God is calling us to mend the holes we have in our nets, which represents our own understanding that has not allowed us to draw people in who need His love and acceptance. He is also calling us to network, just as they had to call over other boats to help with such a large harvest. Immediately after the large fish encounter, Jesus asked them to lay down their nets and follow Him. This is a sacrifice that God is calling people to right now.

This year many people are being called to lay down their own ministries and businesses for a time, and help those that are starting to experience greater favor. The result will expand the Kingdom much more quickly, and it will bring a blessing to those who make the sacrifice. It is time to share Kingdom resources with churches and ministries that are about to emerge.

God wants to open new strategies to us, but we have to let go of the old. It will require many of us to make some radical changes and let go of connections to the past. This might be things that God had called you to in a previous season that is no longer what He is doing now.

Some of you have been holding on to possessions, properties and old ways of doing things that are causing losses in your life. If your finances are hemorrhaging over businesses, purchases, or possessions you are holding on to, it might be time to let them go. This applies also to your ministry style or process.

Dream: Tsunami Coming to Technology

I had a prophetic dream that I was in a high office that overlooked a high-tech area of California. This was not Silicon Valley, but it was similar. It appeared to be Southern California.

Suddenly a tsunami wave came and hit the high-tech companies. I knew this was not literal but a prophetic sign that God's Holy Spirit is moving on technology. Watch for creative ideas, inventions, and Kingdom strategies to come.

Release of Financial Strategies

"I will repay you for the years the locusts have eaten—the great locust and the young locust, the other locusts and the locust swarm—my great army that I sent among you." Joel 2:25

We need to get healed of our money issues and things that hold us back from living a life of blessing, so that we can be free to minister and support God's work. Even

Jesus had to deal with money and support His ministry. Otherwise there would not have been someone in charge of the money (Judas). The apostle Paul used traditional offerings and support for part of his ministry. Later, he funded his efforts as a tent maker.

Walt Disney once said, "We don't make movies to make money, we make money to make more movies." His goal was not to get rich, but instead, to fund his life calling. He influenced the world with his movies. Because he had the right attitude, Disney® is now a multi-billion-dollar business. This is a Kingdom principle that we need today.

Getting Repaid for Losses

Many people have suffered financial losses over the past few years. God is releasing new strategies and abilities to regain finances because the new things that God is calling you to will cost money to do.

God is calling us to something new, but we might be holding things back by doing things according to tradition as opposed to "doing what the Father is doing."

In John 5:19, Jesus said, "*... he can do only what he sees his Father doing ...*"

But many people today are only doing what they see their spiritual fathers or forefathers doing.

This does not allow us to move into new things as God opens them up. Many people are stalled because they keep trying to go back to old ways instead of leading out in the new. As you step into the new things God reveals to you, do not be surprised if people around you do not agree with you.

Those who are preparing and waiting on God will see a new surge of supernatural favor over your relationships and finances. God is aligning you for blessings. It is important to be flexible and ready to take action as it is revealed.

Joseph Anointing Coming on the Scene

This is the time when those who have been set aside by God to help finance new Kingdom projects will come on the scene—just like when Joseph got the strategy from the Lord. These new movements that are coming are going to cost a lot of money to fund because they will be targeted to the poor in spirit, the outcasts, young people and those who do not have much money.

It will cost a lot of money so God is releasing financial strategies and raising up spirit-led philanthropists. God is calling us to something new, but what is holding things back is that we are doing things by habit or tradition as opposed to "doing what the Father is doing."

For example, in Genesis 26 Isaac was going to go to Egypt during the famine like his father did, but God spoke to him and told him to go into the land of the Philistines instead. The result was that he got blessed a hundredfold in a time of famine (Genesis 26:12).

Many people are stalled because of trying to go back to old ways instead of leading out in new. We need to get a new strategy to reach people and to make money to finance what is coming. We also need to break through the spirit of fear and terrorism being spread through the Internet. It is time to short-circuit the plans of the enemy and put in the glory of God!

CHAPTER 9

CLOSING WORDS

"Keep your eyes on Jesus, who both began and finished this race we're in. Study how he did it. Because he never lost sight of where he was headed—that exhilarating finish in and with God—he could put up with anything along the way: Cross, shame, whatever. And now he's there, in the place of honor, right alongside God." Hebrews 12:2 MSG

I encourage you to keep your eyes on Jesus and not on the storms or negative talk that are raging around us. God will be shifting us away from many outdated beliefs and doctrines. These were effective in previous seasons, but they will not work well for us in the new.

We do need to be aware of where we place our focus. Our focus is first and foremost on God and his awesome power and solutions for us. Focusing more on Satan and what is wrong will drain and distract us, which is his goal! He wants us in a constantly stressed state where all we do is troubleshoot and try to fix things.

Whatever we put our attention to starts to becomes our reality, whether it is real or true or not.

Early in my spiritual life, I fell into this trap. It is especially tempting for prophetic people and those with the gift of discerning of spirits. There is a time and place to discern and overcome the plans of Satan. But, putting too much attention on the enemy's plans can get us sidetracked from bringing God's love into a situation.

Ultimately, it is God's Holy Spirit and glory that will shift the spiritual atmosphere over a person or situation. When I was able to grasp this in my life, I switched from seeing demons and negativity to seeing more angels, and prophetic solutions started flowing. The Heavens began to open up more and I was able to step into the ministry I have today.

A solution is to focus on good things and look for God's plans. This is important because "what you sow you shall reap" can work for us in both the positive and the negative.

"Finally, brothers and sisters, whatever is true, whatever is noble, whatever is right, whatever is pure, whatever is lovely, whatever is admirable—if anything is excellent or praiseworthy—think about such things." Philippians 4:8

Get Your Hopes Up

This is a time in which God is giving us an infusion of new hope. Over the past few months, God has been blowing upon the dry bones of prophetic promises that were given to you in the past. These are things that have not come about, or they started and then stopped.

Things have been changing beneath the surface that are now going to spring up with new life. Forgotten promises and prayers from the past are going to be answered. Be open to the answer to your prayers looking different than you may have originally envisioned.

"Now hope does not disappoint, because the love of God has been poured out in our hearts by the Holy Spirit who was given to us." Romans 5:5 NKJV

Many people have stopped hoping for some of these promises because it has been so long in coming. It is safe to hope again. God is healing people with broken hearts and broken spirits!

God is Redeeming Your Bad Experiences

God is the giver of good gifts. He is a loving Father and likes to relate to us as a good Father would with His children. Many have not had a good or positive experience with healthy authority figures. God is doing two things in this time. He is healing our image and understanding of who He really is and He is going to use you, in turn, to help heal others.

"Which of you fathers, if your son asks for a fish, will give him a snake instead? Or if he asks for an egg, will give him a scorpion? If you then, though you are evil, know how to give good gifts to your children, how much more will your Father in heaven give the Holy Spirit to those who ask him!" Luke 11:11–13

If you have suffered pain or losses at a particular time of year, expect God to start redeeming that with you.

For instance, before the Lord healed my life, I had a lot of pain and losses as a child during three particular times of the year—my birthday in March, the anniversaries of my parents' deaths in September and the Christmas season. These often left me feeling depressed.

God has now redeemed these three times of the year in my life. Now I get visitations, fun surprises and huge blessings on all three of these.

God wants to do the same with you. The enemy wants to try to cut off your times of blessings, but God is going to redeem bad seasons.

Love Note from God

This is for you and those who need it:

"I am repaying you for the years of loss, tears and pain. I am taking you to a new level and new friends and connections are going to form around you.

The desires of your heart will unfold more clearly this year than ever before. I am going to surround you with people that are supportive and will help you to breakthrough.

I am positioning you and bringing deeper revelation, wisdom and understanding for this season. I am going to redeem all the pain, suffering, losses and setbacks. I will show you that your suffering on Earth is bringing you greater gain in Heaven.

My love for you is great and I have captured your tears and your cries have not gone unnoticed. A new season is here with greater health, increased healing anointing and energy. Your strength will increase. You will receive financial blessings, as your crossing over will happen fast. I am with you so do not give up."

Get ready for the greatest times that are yet to come. God is still God and He has a plan for us all. This is going to be an amazing year!

ABOUT DOUG

Doug Addison is a prophetic speaker, author and coach. He is known for his *Daily Prophetic Words*, *Spirit Connection* webcast, podcast and blog. Doug's message of love, hope and having fun reaches people around the world! His powerful, positively funny teaching style and coaching helps open people to discover their destiny and experience God's supernatural love and power. He and his wife Linda live in Los Angeles, California where he is impacting the arts, entertainment and media industries.

DougAddison.com

MORE RESOURCES FROM DOUG ADDISON

Hearing the Voice of God 365

Hearing the Voice of God 365 is an online prophetic activation school that comes to you! Through the twelve modules in this school, you will learn to discern the voice of God every day, grow in your gifts, walk in your identity and discover the destiny God has for you!

Hearing the Voice of God 365 is filled with how-to instruction by Doug, along with exclusive mentoring sessions with prophetic leaders including Lance Wallnau, Lana Vawser, Sandi Krakowski and more. It also provides activation exercises designed to help you learn to hear the voice of God, deepen your relationship with Him and save you time!

Learn more at: HearingGod365.com

How to Flip Your Financial Future

This book packs a powerful punch to activate you in practical Kingdom strategies for sowing and reaping, getting out of debt, increasing your income, and even starting or growing your business or ministry, so you can *flip* your financial future ... and flip it good!

God Spoke, Now What?

God is continually speaking to you—sending you messages to help you as you walk through your life journey. Oftentimes, people do not realize when God is speaking to them and they do not know how to interpret and activate the messages they receive. In his book, *God Spoke, Now What? Activating Your Prophetic Word*, Doug Addison not only shows you how to recognize the messages God is sending you through dreams, life experiences, the media, other people or natural circumstances; he also teaches you how to interpret the messages and activate them so you can see breakthroughs happen in your life.

Write Your Book Now! Online Course

Write Your Book Now! is the all-inclusive online course with everything you need to get your book written and published as quickly as possible—without sacrificing quality. Writing a book used to be a long, painful task, but *Write Your Book Now!* helps you accelerate the writing process so you can have a completed manuscript—in as little as 30 days!

Write a Book Quickly: Unlock Your Creative Spirit

Whether you are just starting out or are an experienced writer, this precise book can help you get to a new level. Tap into your creative nature, learn secrets of writing, publishing tips, writing resources, exercises and more.

Personal Development God's Way

People everywhere want to know their life's purpose and destiny. *Personal Development God's Way* was developed after Doug Addison spent a lifetime studying why some people's lives change radically and others do not.

This book is packed full of practical examples, stories and exercises designed to apply to your life.

Spiritual Identity Theft Exposed

The rise of identity theft in the world today parallels what is happening spiritually to people everywhere. People have been blinded to their true identity and the destiny they were created to live.

Spiritual Identify Theft Exposed contains seven strategies from darkness and seven remedies to change your life forever.

Understand Your Dreams Now: Spiritual Dream Interpretation

Doug Addison's *Understand Your Dreams Now: Spiritual Dream Interpretation* is drawn from decades of classroom and real-world experiences.

It contains everything you need to get started or to go to a new level of interpreting dreams. Includes a 300-symbol dream dictionary.

Dream Crash Course Online Training

Understanding dreams does not have to be difficult! Doug Addison is an expert dream interpreter who has interpreted over 25,000 dreams and has trained thousands of dream interpreters worldwide.

He has developed a crash course on how to understand your dreams quickly. This is everything you need in one online program. Includes ten online videos, MP3s, study guide, dream journal, symbols dictionary and more!

Prophetic Tattoo and Piercing Interpretation Online Training

Now you can learn the inside secrets to *Prophetic Tattoo and Piercing Interpretation* from Doug Addison. After years of development, Doug Addison is making this one-of-a-kind online training available to you. Find what you need to get started in this new cutting-edge outreach strategy! This online training includes seven online videos, MP3s, study guide, tattoo reference cards and more.

Visit: DougAddison.store

REFERENCES

[i] Wikipedia contributors. *Yom Kippur* [2.1 Heavenly Books are Opened] *Wikipedia, The Free Encyclopedia.* Retrieved from https://en.wikipedia.org

[ii] Jones, B. (February 2015). *Remembering Bob Jones on His 85th Birthday* [Web post, Prophetic Words, 2015]. Retrieved from http://www.bobjones.org

[iii] Ibid.

[iv] Addison, D. (2015) *2016 Prophetic Forecast* (Santa Maria, CA: InLight Connection).

[v] Jones, B. (February 2011). *The Net* [Web post, Prophetic Words, 2011]. Retrieved from http://bobjones.org